SOCIAL

MARRIAGE

By Elizabeth Yang

I dedicate this book to my mom, Kelly Lili Yang, who has inspired me with her love, strength, and courage to be the committed, integrous, and confident leader I am today.

I also dedicate this book to my husband Philip Cheng, who has been my guinea pig in making this concept of Social Marriage a success.

Last but not least, I dedicate this book to Erika Ruiz, who is an amazing author and has generously guided me through the publishing process.

Table of Contents

PREFACE

Marriage. This topic affects every single human being on the planet. Should I get married or not? When should I get married? What makes a marriage work? Should I divorce?

Marriage is a conversation that was created a long time ago. In the Middle Ages, women needed to get married to own property through their husbands. In today's day and age, the conversations are completely different. Due to the high divorce rates, it's apparent that the benefits that come with legal marriage are far outweighed by the disadvantages that come with it. In California, it can take as little as a day to get married but to get divorced, the minimum time allotted by law is 6 months. That's not even taking into account the expensive court fees, attorney fees, and stress. If a divorce is uncontested, it could take as little as 6 months. If a divorce is contested, there is no time limit, and the case could drag on for years.

More and more people choose not to get married now because they see marriages fail all around them, from parents to siblings to friends. The divorce rate is going down because the marriage rate is going down.

Social Marriage is a new conversation that is being introduced into the world. It's the same as legal marriage but without the legal expectations that come with it and without the possibility of a legal divorce that could follow. The partners can still refer to each other as "husband" and "wife," wedding parties can still be held, engagement photos can still be taken, and wedding bands can still be worn. The only difference is that no marriage license is applied, and no legal marriage document is executed.

This book will go into the many benefits that Social Marriage has to offer, what a strong relationship requires, how commitment does not depend on a piece of paper, and how Social Marriage has helped many people maintain strong relationships that otherwise may have met their demise in a legal marriage.

Chapter 1

THE PROBLEM

~~~⠿⠿⠿⠿⠿~~~

Introduction

We live in a time of instant self-gratification. Just about everything we think we want is within our reach. This includes most things like food, sex, social entertainment, material things, even marriage. We have the advancement in technology to thank for a lot of that. In most states obtaining a marriage license has little requirement other than filling out paperwork. There is even the option of going online to expedite the process. A blood test is required in some cases, but the turnaround time is still 2-3 weeks most of the time. Getting things seems to be easy. But what about getting rid of things, like a failed marriage?

I have found that the problem that exists is two-fold. It involves the legal system and the couple wanting to sever their relationship. According to the Centers for Disease Control and

Prevention (CDC), the marriage rate in 1990 was 7.9% per 1,000 total population in California. The rate dropped to 6.0 in 2018. I believe the drop-in rate is due to millennials being discouraged about what marriage is supposed to be, not just in California but everywhere else in the United States. There just aren't very many role models to show how it is done anymore. Several Family law attorneys' groups have done the research and concluded that almost 50% of marriages in the U.S. would end in divorce or separation, with 41% of first marriages ending in divorce, 60% of second marriages, and 73% of third marriages (https://www.wf-lawyers.com/divorce-statistics-and-facts/). So, it appears the marriage and divorce rate numbers are trending in a downward motion. If the marriage rate increases, then the divorce rate increases. If the marriage rate decreases, then the divorce rate decreases as well.

In this chapter, I share my experience as I feel it illustrates what I believe is the two-fold problem with marriage and divorce and its connection to the legal system. My married life only lasted 1.5 years, but it took much longer than that to get divorced. It took over 4 years. In other words, it was a lot easier for me to get married than to get divorced. In California, where I reside, even if the parties agree on getting divorced and all terms associated, there is still a mandatory six-month waiting period. But, even beyond that, unsettled issues between the couple and the legal system's competence can prolong the severing process.

Once Love Dies

What started out as love for me didn't last long. In fact, it only lasted 1.5 years. Looking back now, I can see the challenges I faced as an opportunity for growth, but when you're face to face with pain, it's hard to see. As an attorney, I provide service for a wide spectrum of clients. Some clients come in stressed about the marriage before it begins. This is due to the assets they are trying to protect through filing for a prenup. At the time of my divorce, I was a lawyer but not practicing. For some, it may seem odd to think about the end before the beginning. I knew things like that existed, but I didn't consider that it was something I should ever need to factor in.

In the beginning, I was in love. I was caught up in a whirlwind of all the possibilities that love brings. Freedom and letting my guard down are not something I had practiced in my early life. Growing up, my mom had high expectations for me, and I had to deliver. There was no slacking on building success or taking time to enjoy simple freedoms that other youth my age were enjoying. At an early age, I had accomplished a lot. Somewhere when deciding that I didn't want to get a master's degree in engineering and decided to go to law school, I granted myself some time for freedom. I found that I was the complete opposite of the child my "Tiger mom" had molded. I loved being "carefree." My carefree liberation led me to meet the man who would be my husband, and he swooped me off my feet. Soon after, I learned that I was pregnant. Try explaining that to a "Tiger mom" who was very engaged in the Chinese culture's traditions. It was a very challenging time for me. My mom stated it was unacceptable to have a baby out of wedlock. I was grateful that the father wanted a child, so we became legally married.

It wasn't until after the birth of our second child years later that I knew something was different. Love blinded me to the warning signs earlier on—the excuses of why he couldn't come home and so on. But as I started looking around, I found evidence that the love I thought we shared had died. Nothing prepares you for that moment. My heart literally ached and hurt. My then-husband admitted his infidelity. Little did I know how the pain and disappointment would benefit me or how the knowledge that I had acquired up to that moment would help me get through what felt like the worst time of my life. In California, there is a six-month cooling-off period when a divorce is filed. This provides time for mediation, re-focusing, or re-thinking your decision. While this works for some couples, it didn't work for our case.

The Reality

My ex-husband and I got legally married, and the marriage ended in betrayal and lies. Even though we had two kids together, made vows, and got a marriage license, there was still no commitment. The reality is we all bring our story to the marriage. When you get the marriage license, nothing magical happens to the relationship. Having a piece of paper does not guarantee a solid or long-lasting marriage. That is something each individual in the marriage decides.

Many questions surfaced for me during this trying time. I pondered the reasons people get married if not for love. It seemed like the "Till death do us part" was a joke. For me, I know that I wasn't all-knowing about life when I got married. I was experiencing freedom as a young adult. I wanted to explore love and be valued by someone who loved me. I never expected that it would end so abruptly. We were only in 1.5 years, and we had two kids. As I mentioned in the beginning, we live in a world where self-gratification is important. It has spilled over into marriage and has lessened the tolerance levels and staying power. In past times, marriages were built on something more solid than getting selfish personal needs met.

Today, couples are not willing to be in a marriage unhappily. They then sever the relationship because they just can't stand it anymore. More millennials are skipping the marriage license and finding other ways to be together. Several articles exist that discuss how the sacred marriage union has lost its thrill. More people are skipping the license while engaging in the roles of husband and wife.

It's hard enough to part ways, but what if assets or children are in the mix? This could make it very difficult when settling matters. As I was deep in my own situation going through my divorce, time passed, and more insult was added to injury as we battled out the end of what started out in love.

A Prolonged Ending

I never expected my divorce to take as long as it did. Divorce is hard enough, so the extended waiting was not helpful. Our fight was over anything and everything: custody of the kids, alimony, assets, and whatever else. I was hurt, and I wanted to make him hurt, too. So, I made things difficult, and he pushed back each time with more difficulty. Our kids were young, but they could feel the tension between us. This went on for more than four years.

We spent a ridiculous amount of money on attorney fees; for me, it was approximately $250,000, for my ex-husband it was approximately $300,000. Also, I went through five different law firms before settling the divorce myself. The core problem presented itself; I had never learned how to resolve conflict. An overall lack of education in conflict resolution is a problem that seems to be ignored or not considered as the culprit for the divorce rates.

It wasn't until I attended a class on emotional intelligence that I realized the knowledge I was missing. My divorce was prolonged partly because I had no clue how to communicate or resolve the conflict between me and my ex-husband. No one teaches this in school at any level. Yet, it is where things fall apart in relationships. I had allowed my hurt to take control. I thought I was doing what it took to protect myself. Four years to get a divorce is way too long, and the stress of it was exhausting. Time was spent trying to plan the next move of how to keep everything in check. Instead, we could have been communicating to reach an agreement. But we chose to fight because neither one of us had been taught a better way. I became certified in mediation because I wanted to help couples learn ways to communicate with each other. Communication, even in a divorce, is not about who is right or wrong. It is about coming to an agreement. To do that, you have to listen fully to what is being said, not to what is in your head. We all have things in our story that cause us to feel or behave a certain way. Understanding emotional intelligence helps with the acceptance of self and the forgiveness process. It teaches you that forgiveness is not just for the other person, but for you to let go so you can move on in peace. I'm not saying it is easy, but it is necessary.

Another problem I realized that prolonged my divorce was the competence level of the lawyers I engaged in helping me. I went through five of them before I just gave up and wrote the petition myself. Papers were spread across my bedroom for a

while as I learned how to best serve myself. Every divorce case is a unique situation and should be treated that way. The best person to help is a lawyer who is knowledgeable about divorce through personal experience. They are more apt to handle your case as if it were their own. I think it's hard for a lawyer who has never experienced a custody battle to understand what to do for you. There is no template of one size fits all. The nuances are too unique for each case.

Going through a divorce is no easy process. The length of time you were married doesn't play a role in how much pain is felt. The severing that takes place still affects your emotions in a way that can't be fully explained, even if you want the divorce. Marriage is a union that has been around since the beginning of time. It has evolved for some into a more casual affair. For others, it still holds the strong ties that bind a couple together forever. The times we live in today have so many options for couples who what to be together. Cultures and religion have their stand on the issue as well. It can be challenging to know what is good and acceptable.

This chapter illustrated the challenges of my own divorce. The next will introduce what came out of my pain. During the process, I learned something about myself and how to effectively communicate with others. In the end, I was able to reach out to my ex-husband and communicate my feelings. My desire was to heal. A lot had happened between us, and we wanted the best for our children. Though we could not be together as a couple, we became friends. And that was the best ending possible for what had been a long fight to freedom for both of us.

Chapter 2

LEARNING THE GAME

Introduction

Going through four years of divorce made an impact on my life. Not only did it teach me something about myself, but it also showed me how far we can be from a life of contentment and happiness with the answer well within our reach. In 2007, I transitioned from engineering into law. When I started out practicing law, my focus was on patents, trademarks, and copyrights. My focus changed again in 2010, the year I filed for my divorce. I did the initial paperwork myself through trial and error. I didn't do a very good job because I knew nothing about family law at the time. I ended up going through five different law firms and was pretty unhappy with each of them. The reason for my success in Family Law today is because of my four years of experience working on my own case. I finalized my divorce in 2014. Family law is not just something you learn overnight. I am convinced that experience is the best teacher.

In this chapter, I share my journey of building knowledge in the specialty of Family Law while going through four years of divorce. I became very well-versed with the industry and now practice as a Family Law attorney, dealing daily with divorces, prenups, postnups, child custody, child support, asset division, and countless other disputes. I feel that it's pretty disheartening that the divorce rate in Los Angeles, California, is now over 60%. My motivation to change my own situation for the better has driven me to contribute something positive as a resolution to what used to be considered a sacred union between two individuals who truly loved one another, in something known as marriage.

The Problem I See

Awareness of the problems, for me, began with what was happening in my situation. Going through a divorce is a very emotional time. A divorce is one of the worst things you can go through. It's right up there with death and taxes. I was super emotional as I worked through the layers of my divorce. It became where I could not focus on anything, not even on my own cases. The lawyers I employed were not helpful. They were just charging me money without delivering the service I requested. The game behind the scenes was not clear to me at first. It was only when I stopped trying to win and focused on healing that I could see it clearly.

The first problem I saw was with the lawyers. One of the lawyers forgot to submit my witness list, something key to my case. At the foundational level of family law, there's this conflict of interest that exists. If a lawyer settles your case, then they don't make any more money. There is no way around it because you have to get a lawyer. The reality is most will not act in your best interest. No winner comes out of it, but definitely a fee.

The second problem was me. I wanted to win many things during the process, basically whatever was on the table or thrown at me next. I learned that that kind of mindset wasn't going to get me anywhere. It left me feeling stressed and exhausted, trying to plan my next move. Healing and resolution were winning on a different level, and I accepted that.

I realized somewhat late in the course of my four-year divorce marathon that I needed mediation. It also became clear how helpful it would be for others as well. My need for mediation came from the depths of the pain I was experiencing and my desire for closure. That was me as the client. As the attorney, I desire to free individuals from the stress and help them reach an agreement quickly. With my divorce, it finally took mediation and settlement for it to finalize. That's why I wanted to go into family law: because I wanted to help people avoid going through what I went through, and potentially wasting their money and time without getting a resolution.

In my firm, we are called Law Mediation Officers. I specialize in handling cases of child support and custody, alimony, division of debts, domestic violence, and restraining orders, as well as prenups and postnups. Along with divorce, all of these cases could benefit from mediation. The first thing I do when I talk to a client is to offer mediation. Mediation is defined as an intervention to help resolve a dispute. The majority of the clients I serve are going through a divorce. Either they do not understand the process or cannot reach an agreement on various issues. I come in as either an attorney or a mediator to help them resolve their family law issues. I also have clients that I serve who are planning on getting married and, in those instances, I assist them with their pre-nuptial agreements.

I always advise my clients that mediation is the better route over litigation. If they go to court, the judge presiding over their case has no idea what their lives are like. This judge, who is a stranger to their daily lives, has the authority to create a court order after only listening to each side for a limited time. Both parties will then have to obey that court order moving forward. From my experience, whenever a judge creates an order, both parties usually do not like the order. Still, they must follow it as it is legally binding.

Before mediation begins, I like my clients to understand that there are no guarantees because its success or failure depends entirely on the client. The following points are the techniques and considerations used in the mediation process.

■ The Talking Stick

This is an active listening exercise. The person who has the stick has the right to speak. The person not holding the stick is not allowed to speak. If either one of them violates the rule, they lose a point. With communication as the goal, the person listening is only to respond to what they hear. If they get it correct, then it would be the other person's turn. For example, when the husband spoke, his wife had to first say what she heard instead of responding and talking over him. She could only respond if she heard correctly. He might say, "I feel like you're not honest and truthful with me," and she would respond with, "I heard you say that I'm not communicating with you. Is that accurate?" If he says yes, then it would be her turn to speak.

Once they understand each other, they can come to an agreement. I then just have to draft the papers. The divorce can happen sooner, or they can get on with their lives together, incorporating the communication techniques learned. Sometimes this can take a lot of time when there are layers and layers of misunderstandings. The reason people like mediation is it allows each person to be heard. The ego doesn't have to be right. One thing I like to have couples do before they come for mediation is to write down what they want to achieve out of the mediation. At the end of the mediation, I have them write down what they agreed on and sign it. That way, they leave on the same page.

■ The Love Language

I like to also include the different love languages of couples. There are five love languages that human beings can utilize to give and receive love:

- Quality time
- Physical touch
- Words of affirmation
- Acts of service
- Gifts

All individuals have different preferences in terms of giving and receiving love. Usually, when they have a primary love language they prefer to receive, they will use that type of love language to express their love. However, if their partner does not share the same primary love language, no matter how much they feel like they're expressing love, their partner may not feel loved nor receive it. Some people looking on might object to how a person in the marriage could file for divorce when they seem to be receiving love from the other. But they don't realize there was a disparity in the love languages. When each individual can discover both their own preferred love language and their partner's, they will be able to love their partner the way that their partner wants to be loved; hence, resolving a lot of conflicts in the process.

One tip I will leave with you: don't get third parties involved, like mom or other family members. It just makes things complicated. Believe me, you can get through this on your own with the help of the mediator.

A Law For Every Problem

During my education, I have learned about the many disputes couples can have. I will emphasize that though many couples have these disputes, each dispute will be a unique situation. Couples seeking legal assistance must understand the concept of "one size does not fit all." Their case may have the same title as someone else's, but it should be handled in a way that fits their unique needs and issues.

3 Top Disputes

■ Finances

Finances is a big one. This involves the distribution of the assets and debt. Everything obtained in the marriage is community property, no matter if it's under one person's name. Every state is different, but California has this law. It doesn't matter who makes money in the marriage; it belongs to both parties. Every state is different. Some have similar property laws.

■ **Alimony**

Spousal Support or Alimony in California is calculated by a calculator called DissoMaster, created by the government. The length of time you receive alimony depends on the number of years you were married. There is a long term marriage, where you have been married longer than 10 years, which equals a lifetime of spousal support. Then there is the short-term marriage, which is considered being married 5 years or less. An amount is calculated based on the numbers provided for income from both parties. Alimony does stop once the person receiving the support re-marries.

■ **Prenups**

There is no such thing as a bulletproof prenup. Legal marriage is a huge risk for those with lots of money. The problem with prenups is that no judge looks at it until it's needed. And it's only needed if going through a divorce. At that time, the judge evaluates it and decides if it is acceptable for the couple's situation. That is the risk you take getting one.

The challenge of the whole prenup discussion is it is not very romantic. Marriage is supposed to be a special time in life; drawing up prenup financial papers creates the seeds of doubt. This can make the process stressful for each person. The person who has the money wonders if the person will understand them getting the prenup, but the person who doesn't have the money wonders if they think they are marrying them for their money and may feel some kind of way about that.

*Child support and child custody issues are a different deal. I leave them out of the discussion here on purpose. That is something that would need to be settled with or without marriage.

The Numbers Talk

Divorce rates were rising but have decreased due to millennials having a different view about marriage and how it fits with their lifestyle. Some don't want to get married until they are stable in their finances, accomplish some goals, and figure life out. This raises some interesting questions about the reasons to get married.

A look back at history shows that marriage has evolved into something less scary than it started out to be. From the biblical sense, marriage is a sacred institution and should be respected. It was said that the man and woman would join together to be one flesh. Now, even in that, there is much controversy. But the ideal and meaning of marriage are what I'm talking about. It is important to note that some cultures are still engaged in following their practices concerning marriage. There was also a time when women couldn't own property, so they had to have it through their husbands. It is said that marriage came from middle English, 1250-1300 CE. In those times, marriage had different goals other than love attached to it. It was focused on the alliance between families, economic liaisons; it wasn't about love. So, this begs the question, "How long has love and commitment been lacking from marriage?"

Today, people are not getting married, but they are getting together in different ways to meet their personal, financial, and social needs. It seems that legal marriage is outdated, at least by the standards most of us have thought of it. It seems that socially married people are more committed than legally married people. The divorce rates are evidence that people don't take legal marriage seriously. Infidelity is high in a legal marriage. The minute the couple has a disagreement, they argue and are finished with the marriage. There is no staying power. Commitment and love are not proportionally related to legal marriage at all. In the next chapter, I propose a solution to what seems to be a lost art: marriage.

Chapter 3

THE SOLUTION: SOCIAL MARRIAGE

—⁂—

Introduction

Sometimes the best solutions are the simple ones. In this chapter, I introduce my solution to the problem of legal marriage and then divorce: "Social Marriage." Just like with any new concept, there is some resistance. After much thought after my four-year-long divorce, I reflected on the idea of "Social Marriage." It is basically the same as a legal marriage, except the couple does not apply for or sign a marriage license. Though my solution seems simple, it is not traditional. There are those people, most of them not millennials, that feel legal marriage and having children is the goal of life. With all the uncertainty it presents, it nevertheless is a high priority in some peoples' minds.

Social Marriage strips away all the formalities and allows the couple to commit to each other in their own way and in their own timeframe. The pressures are real in societies, families, and even with our own expectations about how we should be and what things are acceptable to do. Legal marriage does not guarantee that the love the couple starts out with will last forever till death do them part. It does not make the marriage free of infidelity. My point is there is more to be considered than a piece of paper that says you are husband and wife. As without it, legal marriage has a long history of being something to achieve.

Perhaps the attraction of financial benefits for married couples is enough to make them marry the traditional way. According to TurboTax, married couples have 7 tax advantages: the couples' tax bracket could be lower together, a spouse may be a tax shelter; a jobless spouse can have an IRA; couples may "benefit shop; " a married couple can get greater charitable contribution deductions; marriage can protect the estate; and filing can take less time and expense. There are also other perks for married people set up by the government, like the cost of insurance policies - costing less than they do for a single person - and the distribution of money in social security or other accounts that go to your loved ones after you die. If you are single, your money goes back to the system. The question remains whether or not the government favors traditional marriage, which matters most when two people decide to be committed to each other. I can tell you: it is not the signed marriage license. The divorce rates prove that.

A Paperless Marriage

A paperless marriage is basically the same as a legal marriage, except it does not require a signed contract or license. It gets rid of the assumptions made by the law that just because you are married means everything you own and acquire becomes community property. While my solution is less known, I feel it takes the bulk of the stress out of the relationship and separation or divorce process. It allows the couple to focus on communication, love, and other pieces that build the relationship. If the couple chooses to have all the things that a legal marriage has minus the contract, it is possible. Social Marriage forces couples to communicate and be intentional with everything they do together, which means having joint bank accounts, buying property, having kids and raising them, to name only a few. The couple can still live together and share expenses, but on their own terms. Social Marriage offers that what is yours is truly yours, and that means your credit can remain good even if your partner ruins theirs through poor money management or some other reason. One thing my experience has taught me is that life is too short. We have the power to create the life we want, yet no matter what, we still cannot control anybody else. This means for the very best outcomes, we must be realistic and intentional, and most importantly, self-aware. My purpose is not to dismiss legal marriage as something unreasonable. I am sure there are some married couples that do it well. My hope is to present another option for couples who want marriage but without the license, which we know does not equal more commitment.

Steps to Social Marriage

The steps to Social Marriage are not really that different from things done in a legal marriage. View the following steps to see how they are similar.

■ Dating

Most relationships begin with dating. It starts with two people falling for each other. As the relationship develops, they agree to be exclusive. Taking the relationship to the next level can feel exciting, but it is important to think about what that means and if you are ready for it. The dating level is a good place to practice thinking about what you really want out of a relationship. As time goes on, more feelings and emotions are invested, and it is important to know where you stand now.

■ The Proposal

Everyone loves a good proposal. Just because you opt for a Social Marriage does not mean you cannot experience getting proposed to or proposing to the one you love. The proposal can be as grand (or not) as you like it.

■ Fiancé Stage

I like to think of this stage as the planning stage. So much preparation can go into planning your lives together. Most traditional couples use this time to set a date for their wedding and start planning for it. It is the couple's prerogative in what they want to do. During this stage, I feel it is good to get marriage counseling. Some religions enforce counseling even in legal marriages. I know the Catholic religion requires it. Just like in dating, clarity is important. Marriage counseling is beneficial because it provides needed education on marriage, and it allows couples to communicate and discuss their goals with each other.

I recommend counseling throughout the marriage. I like to think of it as an intervention or maintenance for the relationship that keeps the couple focused on communicating with each other. Some people think that you only go to counseling when something is wrong, but that is far from the truth. When you are the happiest and healthy, counseling can be helpful at keeping you on the same page. I have found that everybody has blind spots. There are also books to read with different topics concerning all things that have to do with marriage, from having kids to being a stay-at-home mom or dad. Other options include games the couple can play where they can ask each other questions.

■ The Wedding

The wedding for Social Marriage is the climax, just like it is for legal marriage. Showing your commitment is dependent on how creative you want to be. There is always the option of how you choose to communicate your devotion to your significant other. Some couples like to stick with the traditional ring exchange while others choose to do nothing. Some skip the whole wedding celebration and travel somewhere for the honeymoon. They pick a day to be husband and wife, and that becomes their anniversary date. Keep in mind, if couples want to create their own contract and sign it that is up to them.

Let Go of Tradition

History, family, and culture have informed us that certain things must take place to be married. Couples can already be unique in how they communicate and show intimacy to each other, so when the expectation from family or culture is factored in, things can get difficult. The Chinese culture in past generations engaged in arranged marriages. It was important to marry in the same social class. Though things are changing, some still hold on to this tradition. The same goes for other countries like Africa. They are very tribalistic. For some, it is good to marry someone within your own tribe. Besides all the arranged marriages and social class requirements, there are still families in the U.S. that believe you are not married until you walk down the aisle and say your wedding vows to each other.

Social Marriage lets go of tradition. Compared to traditional marriage, it probably sounds strange. I get that; it does sound too good to be true that you can be committed and live with someone without the marriage license. I have found that we hang on to so many things that perceive to have value but are not important enough to settle for unhappiness. I got married for the first time for the wrong reason. There I was, pregnant and not married. That was not okay for my Chinese culture. So, we got married. About a year later, the marriage was over. It took longer to dissolve the marriage than to get married. I reacted to the pressure of my mom.

If you choose to give in to the tradition of legal marriage, be ready for what comes next. When families achieve their goals of convincing you to get married next, they expect you to have kids. In social marriage, you determine when everything happens, even when you start calling each other husband and wife as well as when you will have kids. Unfortunately, there have been times when people have gotten abortions because they did not want to have a baby out of wedlock. Again, Social Marriage allows for thinking through difficult situations with logic, considering your feelings and not what is expected of you by others.

Dealing with family can be difficult. Though it is your life and your decision, they can make it hard for you to feel good about your choice, mainly because they want something else for you. It takes a strong person to stand firm against something that has been around for generations. It is never about which is better or worse, but about what works for you.

In Chinese culture, they are very traditional. Even prenups are not popular. But now they are warming up to the idea. Wealthy families love the idea of a prenup because they do not have to worry about protecting the trust they have for their children. Keep in mind, whatever you do has to make sense for you as a couple. I have not known anyone to request to see your marriage license. Most people just assume you are husband and wife if you call each other that. Who really knows who is legally married. You can even have the same last name and not be legally married. It is just a process whenever you decide to do it.

To Be or Not to Be

With Social Marriage, when it is time to call it quits, you just go your separate ways, no paperwork involved. It may seem harsh or clean-cut, but it is the no-stress benefit of Social Marriage, at least on the financial side of it. I should mention that if you share assets, then there is the work of selling or splitting them. There is still the requirement of child support if children are in the picture. So, in that respect, it looks like a legal marriage.

Breaking up is never easy. Divorce is the worst; ask anybody that has gone through it. One thing I like about Social Marriage is that it makes couples say what they mean. There are times in arguments where the threat of divorce comes up. Not only does this make the other person feel hurt, but it is also said knowing that divorce is a process and cannot be easily done in the tone that it is said. With Social Marriage, the couple cannot randomly throw out the divorce card when they argue because there is no such thing. If you really want to leave, pack your bags, and leave.

The process of going your separate ways from a Social Marriage is not without some grief. The reality is there is always a cost or consequence to whatever you do. My solution is a less stressful way. It eliminates the paperwork, arguing over possessions, and talking about who did more or less. That is why I recommend communicating through the whole marriage about everything. No one can part feeling uninformed. The hardest part will be saying good-bye. In chapter 6, I will go into more detail on the topic along with other things to consider. But for the next, I hope to convince you that being together in a very meaningful way does not have to be sacrificed for Social Marriage. In fact, it is welcomed.

Chapter 4

TOGETHERNESS

———————— ◦◦◦◦◦—◦◦◦◦◦ ————————

Introduction

In my previous chapter, I introduced you to a new concept called "Social Marriage." In this chapter, I want to explain how couples can be together and share the same things in a Social Marriage as couples in a legal marriage. I would also like to emphasize that being together is more than a legal situation. I feel the term togetherness sometimes refers to having assets or things together more so than being on one accord in the relationship itself. Togetherness can be thought of in varied ways for every individual. There is no right or wrong way to think of it if all roads lead to an understanding that both people in the relationship agree on. Remember, social marriage is supposed to make being together less stressful because there is no focus on who owns what, or who will get what, if the relationship ends.

Choosing that special someone to be with in a committed relationship means understanding the value you each bring and want to share together. The consideration of honesty, fairness, and building something should be a part of the agreement marriage license or not. My experience has taught me that there are more important things in life to focus on than misunderstandings. That is what makes Social Marriage different; nothing is assumed. Everything is discussed. The nature of togetherness really is up to the couple in the relationship. Their responses to each other, behaviors, feelings, thoughts, and commitment will flow from what is in each of their hearts. I recently read a quote that resonated with me. It read,

"Relationships are a process of proving that you are there for one another."

I believe this to be true. People are quick to think that the relationship is all about them when it is about their commitment to the one they claim to love.

41

Togetherness, More Than Feelings

Some people think that being in love is feeling butterflies in your stomach all the time. But that is far from the truth. Ask anyone who is truly in love, and their commitment has stood the test of time and trials. The truth is, being in love is a choice. You get to wake up and choose to love every day. Feelings are not reliable; they come and go. They could be based on anything, hormones, fear, anger, joy, or environmental events. This is where things could get really complicated, especially when decisions are made based on feelings and not facts.

There is no stability in feelings; they will have you all over the place. The term 'pathetic fallacy' illustrates how feelings change. Pathetic fallacy is described as human feelings in response to details in nature; weather is a good example. Some of us do this without thought. When the weather is sunny and warm, we are energetic and happy. Then when the weather is rainy or cloudy, we may tend to feel sad or down. I say these are feelings that you cannot control because we cannot control the weather. It really just shows how unpredictable feelings are. It comes down to commitment. Knowing what your commitment is, allows you to disregard your feeling and move towards continuing in love. So even if you are moody or upset with your significant other, you would still commit to loving them.

Regardless of how you feel, you choose to be with the person you love until you do not feel the love anymore. The butterflies you felt when you first met do not last forever. If you put that kind of pressure on someone to create the butterflies consistently, that is not fair, and you are setting them up for failure because that is not how love works. Love is about giving to that person, not about what to expect. Being committed to be together is like any other goal you set and put effort into. It could be caring for your children, achieving something at work, or anything else. If the goal is important enough, you are committed even when you do not feel like it.

■ Emotional Bank Account

I learned about the emotional bank account from a seminar I attended. The presenter talked about how the 5 love languages - words of affirmation, acts of service, receiving gifts, quality time, and physical touch - relates to it. How you love someone should be based on their love language, the way they want to experience love. In the emotional bank account, you must make the right kinds of deposits to count in raising the balance of the bank account. So, for example, if your significant other had the love language of quality time, you would spend time with him or her to demonstrate your love. If you went out and bought gifts hoping it would take the place of you spending time, that will not count. Doing this consistently over time could deplete your emotional bank account. The challenge is to speak the same language. Have a healthy balance. Five love languages tie into this bank account. You have to deposit the right thing into the bank. When you feel good, you can do things to increase the balance like something the other person would appreciate; do their dry cleaning or do breakfast in bed. This can help during those times when you are in a mood and snap at the other person, decreasing the balance. It is still okay because the account is at a healthy level.

Sometimes the love is stronger for couples because they are focused on togetherness. Some say the vows "Till Death Do Us Part," and there is no meaning in it for them. The relationship starts off being an empty promise because they are only saying the vows as part of the tradition. So, nothing is grounded or has roots in the relationship, which makes it easy to engage in acts of infidelity because the promise made with their mouth was not based on a conscious choice of being together and what that means. Togetherness has to be a choice made with the heart before you even walk down the aisle. If it does not resonate as an everyday choice for them, then they may do something else.

Some people think if they sacrifice so much for their significant other, they are really loving or giving a lot. But sacrifice has a negative connotation that is not parallel with loving unconditionally. It only brings about negative feelings. Those who care about you feel guilty for making you lose out on something so they can have something. Whatever you give should come from an abundance, not a loss.

Living Together

There is such a thing as common law marriage in some states. This is another option people choose to be together, without a legal contract. It is important to check the state you are living in before pursuing to be sure they acknowledge it. I know California is not a state that allows common law marriage. There has been some misunderstanding about what common law marriage is exactly. Some people believe that if you live with a person for a long time, that makes you automatically married, allowing you the same rights and responsibilities as a couple who has been legally married. This is not true. To be considered having a common law marriage, you must hold yourself out there to be married to friends, family, and community, except there is no wedding ceremony. This can be done by the couple calling each other husband or wife, file a joint tax return, use the same last name, sharing an expense, or having a joint bank account. Currently, there are ten states, including the District of Columbia, that recognize common law marriage. Another six states recognize it but have restrictions. There is another step that can be taken to prove your common law marriage. It is called an affidavit of marriage. It can be used as a sworn oath that the marriage is valid. This document can be created, downloaded, and printed online.

I do not know how known it is, but to end a common law marriage is the same as ending a licensed marriage. The couple would need to go through the steps of filing a divorce, even though they never got traditionally married. The same issues, such as division of property, custody, child, and spousal support, would need to be handled. I know this can seem like a lot to go through, but if you were getting any type of benefit from the government, like with taxes while married, then the government wants you to go through the process of dissolving the marriage through divorce.

This is another difference between common law marriage and Social Marriage. There is the assumption of community property with common law marriage without even having a conversation about it. Thus, when the couple wants to go their separate ways, they cannot just walk away. There must be a divorce settlement. Social Marriage offers better transparency. There are no assumptions. Everything taken on is done intentionally. If the couple decides to dissolve the relationship, they can settle it themselves without the legal system.

Another thing worth mentioning is taking care of the disbursement of your assets before you die. Social Marriage creates the need to have a will and list the specifics of it. This is a negative piece of Social Marriage; if you die without a will, your spouse will not get anything. So, the couple needs to make a will and be specific about who gets what.

Sharing Expenses

Sharing expenses is something anyone can do, friends, family, and college roommates. It just involves an understanding of what the parties are agreeing on. This is something that can be decided in a variety of ways. Because it is dealing with expenses, no written contract is needed.

Couples do not need to be legally married to share property. In fact, you can share property no matter what the relationship is. Sharing expenses or property is just a matter of agreement. Anything you agree on, you have to honor that. Couples are forced to communicate about finances in Social Marriage. Because there are no assumptions, something has to be arranged. Different arrangements can be made; everything does not have to be 50/50. Sit down and discuss what works for you two. While monthly expenses like groceries, gas, or electric bills do not need a written contract, I recommend having one for anything that has a title, like a house.

Finances have a way of causing tension in relationships. That is why communication is key. I like to remind couples that putting your money together in one pot is not a sign of your commitment. It is a decision, only. Again, togetherness is more than money. It has to do with being there for the one you love.

Having a Joint Account

Sharing accounts is possible. It is just a matter of paperwork and the requirements of the institutions. In a Social Marriage, it is only a joint account if you decide it is. It is not assumed to be a community property just because you are together. There is always communication if you have an account of how much each of you will put in.

There are pros and cons to sharing a joint bank account. It is wise to know what you are getting into from the start. Be familiar with the rules of the bank and what it means for taxes. Go in fully knowing why you need a joint account. Though it may seem easier as a way to pay household bills, it really is not. It all comes to preferences and choices you make in how to manage to live together. The real challenge is understanding how to not make money or assets a bigger thing than they are. There is the thought that you do not want to lose something you worked so hard for; that is why everything you do is a conversation. Just be careful that finances are not used to prove your love or commitment.

In conclusion, there is togetherness, and then there is taking care of business. In a Social Marriage, you can have a great relationship where you share things, or not. When the focus is taken off who is getting over on the other person or trying to make sure you are not being taken advantage of, you just might start to enjoy one another. The hope always is that the love and commitment you have for each other will win.

Still, there are other things to consider that will be introduced in the next chapter. We all gain an understanding of what things mean from somewhere. To love fully and trust without question does not come easily for some. Some of those reasons come from our culture and family. To learn more, meet me in the next chapter.

Chapter 5

INTERPRETATION

―――――――――――― ⅏―⅏ ――――――――――――

Introduction

Our lives are the sum of interpretations that come from what we believe to be true. If something or someone conflicts with that belief system, they are most likely pushed away. When two people decide to be together in a Social Marriage or otherwise, understanding each other's interpretation is necessary to really know what they are getting into. In this chapter, my aim is to dig a little deeper into relationship issues. I want to address things beneath the surface and why they cause conflict. You are on the right path just by reading this book. Most people like to be in their comfort zone, so anything that makes them uncomfortable is conflicting. Here I challenge you to get uncomfortable as a way to feel comfortable. Keep reading; it will make sense later.

One of the main lessons taught in the transformation classes that I had taken stated that everything in life is an interpretation. After thinking about it for a moment, it made sense. Then the lesson continued to add, everything is a conversation, even that philosophy of itself is a conversation. This means if it is a conversation, it can be changed and shifted, right? There was an example given that relates to how some things in our lives go back to our interpretation of our mom and dad. You could have siblings that grow up in the same household but turn out completely different. One sibling may say, "I had the greatest mom and dad, and they really took care of me." The other sibling says, "I had the worst mom and dad, and they didn't give me any love or affection." Which sibling do you think is right? The correct answer is neither of them is right nor wrong. This is because human beings don't have access to absolute truth. Absolute truth is discovered, not invented, according to the literature out there. Can a square be a triangle or a circle? A square can only be a square. So, with the siblings, it comes down to their interpretations. You could put a child in the perfect family, and they will grow up and complain that they had the worst parents because they weren't allowed to watch tv. It is the child's interpretation of the situation. In a relationship, if the belief is held that it is just a conversation when issues arise, then all you got to do is shift the conversation to one that serves you.

I want people to see that if they see life as an interpretation, they can put their own meaning on anything. Some people put a lot of meaning on the marriage license because it is a legal document, and they put just as much meaning for their marriage vows. Then others put a lot of meaning into what the marriage license means but not their vows. These people may be more likely to have affairs and end up in divorce. Commitment based on external factors is more apt to fall away. When the commitment is internal, from the heart, you don't need anything to make you stay. Vows are just words, and people break their word all the time. Your decision is not based on what other people did or what the government system requires.

Communication

The incorporation of communication techniques can help understand and break down the barriers where differences originate for the couple. I feel education is important and not just the education you get in primary school or college. Each of those lacks information that prepares you for the things you will come up against in life. It would be nice to have classes or training leading up to the marriage that prepare the couple for a long-term relationship.

Communication is the most important part of solving any issues or differences. It is the glue that keeps everything connected and open at the same time. Part of the discovery is to figure out what the real conversation being had is actually about. Some techniques can be used to help with communication. Some of them you may have heard of already.

The thing to remember is that they can only help if they are used.

■ Active Listening

First, it is good to know the purpose of active listening. It is not just to get your point across to the other person; it is to be understood as well. Both people must listen to each other but not for the reason of offering your opinion. With active listening, one person will say something, and the other person has to repeat what they heard before responding. The other person has to respond with what they heard correctly before they respond with what they want to say about what the first person said. This process is repeated until there is an understanding.

■ Think Before You Speak

Sometimes your words can get away from you if you are not careful. When you are emotional or angry, it is good to think before you speak. It is possible to say something you don't mean, and once the words are out there, you can't take them back.

■ No Talking at the Same Time

When two people are talking at the same time, who is listening? The point of communication to hear each other. For progress to be made, you need to hear more than a word here or there. It is better to wait and allow the other person to complete their thought, then at least you listened to something more complete.

■ Do Not Interrupt

Have patience. Communication takes time. You will have your chance to say something. Constantly interrupting each other only prolongs reaching an understanding. To interrupt does not show that you value what the other person is saying.

Getting On The Same Page

Getting on the same page is a process of venturing, so to speak, to the dark side. If you believe that everything we believe comes from somewhere, it is worth finding out where that is. Then perhaps a new interpretation can be made. There are skills and tools that can be used to help the couple get on one accord. At the beginning of relationships, things can be camouflaged. The experience can seem like a fairytale moment until a conflict is encountered. If the couple doesn't have the tools to navigate them through the process of conflict resolution, it could mean continued problems or a breakup.

With interpretation, no one is right or wrong. Differences do not have to matter between couples. As long as they understand each other, they can get on the same page. It's all about understanding each other's interpretations. Often, when things conflict with something we believe in, we tend to push it away. The challenge I'm presenting is not pushing it away, instead finding a way to understand, create new meaning, and focus on the love you have for each other.

Several real-life examples illustrate how people live out their beliefs. Examine the ones below:

- **Example 1:** A person has a certain interpretation of themself, and someone comes up to them and says, "You are so amazing and beautiful". The response might be, "What are you on?" because they don't have that interpretation of themself. Any interpretation that comes their way that doesn't match their belief system of themself will get pushed away. No matter how many compliments they get, they don't accept it because it is not how they believe.

- **Example 2:** A person's interpretation is a feeling of unworthiness, and someone comes along and treats the person like a princess. This causes a problem; there is too much conflict internally. Then another person comes and treats them mediocre, and they connect more with this person because at last somebody gets them.

- **Example 3:** This example deals with the salary. People are going to make the amount of money that they believe they are worth. If person A believes she can only make a small amount of money, then she will only accept a little. Meanwhile, person B believes she is worth a lot, then she will most likely attract and accept a lot. What you believe goes hand and hand with the law of attraction. The law of attraction connects with what is in your mind. The power of belief is what causes you to attract what you believe in.

- **Example 4:** Concerning domestic violence victims, it is stated in the literature that they return to their abusers seven times before they stay gone for good. Why is that? It is their interpretation of who they are and what they deserve. Domestic violence victims keep going back to their abusers because they feel they deserve it, and that is what they believe their life should be like. It is hard to get out of that cycle; they need a lot of support and a transformation of their belief to think about it differently.

- **Example 5:** The Indian culture has the interpretation that their practice of arranged marriages is successful. One of the reasons being that the elders and parents of the young couple are the ones that find the suitable mate that both families can respect and be happy with. It is reported that a high percentage of young people prefer arranged marriages. Indians have the lowest divorce rate in the world. In 2007 it was reported that 1 in 100 Indian marriages ended in divorce. Indians believe that just because the families know each other, it will create a good long-term marriage and relationship.

Just like things evolve in the environment around us, we do too. In relationships, it is important to check in with each other to be sure you are still on the same page. Because couples have different personalities and may be at a different place in their lives, it is a continual process of keeping up with each other's changes. This is true even for couples who get along well. They need to be sure they continue on the same page. Because each person has different ambitions, it is crucial.

The Desire To Grow

For togetherness to flow in harmony, each person has to have a desire to grow. Growth can go in a positive direction where the couple develops and expands their knowledge, even explore outside of their comfort zone. Growth can also go in a negative direction where it leads to nowhere, and eventually, the relationship suffers. Evolution does take place in our lives at certain points. The couple is responsible for checking in with each other to make sure they are still on the same page.

Growth must first start in learning about each other. This can be a fun and exciting experience. The benefit is understanding each other's interpretation of their life, therefore their beliefs. This awareness space should be a safe place for the couple to share and get to know each other. Keep the communication line open; this is a space you may visit more than once.

It is also important to have a desire to grow in other areas of your life. The know-it-all mentality will get you nowhere. Your desire to grow will expand your knowledge and way of thinking, which can stimulate your curiosity and invite other opportunities. This way of thinking is what separates the very successful from those who stagnate. The results prove it. Even Einstein, after all he did, continued to learn. The ambitious seek out ways to nurture their minds and contribute to the whole of society. For relationships to thrive and get past differences and conflict, sometimes counseling is needed. Some people have a problem with counseling because they connect it with something negative, but think about it; is your relationship worth saving? For those who finished reading this chapter, you took the first step to learning something or being reminded of how to hang in there. Continue to educate yourself through reading, training, and communicating with the one you love. The good thing is this can be done without a marriage license. All you need is a committed heart.

There are times when the best hope and strongest desires to make a relationship work are not enough. The option of walking away in the least stressful manner is introduced in the next chapter. There I will share another way Social Marriage can help you remain intact in a not-so-good situation.

Chapter 6

JUST WALK AWAY

———— ⊶⊷⊶ ————

Introduction

Going through a breakup is emotionally tough enough without adding the months of paperwork from a divorce. When I went through my divorce, I initially did the paperwork myself. I was already an attorney before my divorce; I just wasn't practicing family law at the time. I had the option of hiring a lawyer to file the paperwork for me or filing it myself. Thinking I could figure out filling out some forms, I was confident that I could handle it. As I engrossed myself in work, I began to realize how complicated the process actually was. I was just filling out the forms and not really knowing the repercussions and what came next. So, I ended up messing everything up and had to hire an attorney to fix it and take overdoing the paperwork for me. Hiring an attorney can cost a lot of money. Their retainer fee is about $5000. That was in addition to the moving out and other expenses that came with the divorce process. The divorce paperwork just adds oil to the fire.

There is no marriage license in a Social Marriage, so the relationship can be dissolved without legal input in most cases. Of course, it depends on how well everything was communicated between the couple concerning the property or other assets. Things don't have to get messy unless someone is out for revenge. I don't like bringing children into the discussion as something that makes the process easier or more difficult because child support takes place with or without the couple being married. The term palimony does fit into the conversation, though. Even though it is not as popular as alimony, it is something to consider.

My intention with this chapter is to shed some light on what happens on the surface of a dissolved relationship and how there is an internal breaking away that takes place. None of it is easy; I'm not here to convince you of that. Social Marriage offers an advantage because the legal documents burden and the process of communicating to file the paperwork are omitted. Like I said, there is enough emotional hurt to deal with without the added burden of paperwork.

Dealing With The Hurt

In a relationship where you have invested time, trust, and emotions, it is normal to experience hurt feelings when the relationship falls apart. This is true whether there is a marriage license or not. There is a part of breaking up by divorce or just walking away from the Social Marriage that can leave you in a vulnerable and low state. It is important that your coping be done in the most non-threatening, nonanxiety-producing, and sustainable way. A breakup has the potential to change up a lot in your life. Your day-to-day routine is different, you may feel uncertain about your future, or your responsibilities may change. This is normal and the result of experiencing a loss. We all have our way of dealing with hurt. But I think it is good to have some other tools or tips to reach for when you need to.

The first step is to know yourself and how you handle difficult situations. They say divorce is one of the hardest things you can go through, whether or not you wanted it. There is something about cutting the ties of a relationship that hurts bad. Though it hurts while you are going through it, there is hope, and you can heal. For healing to take place, you must be intentional with what you do. Drinking excessive amounts of alcohol may numb the pain for a moment, but when you become sober, the hurt will still be there. So, choosing something that helps you recover is the healthiest option. Just remember to be considerate of yourself and the delicate situation you are in. Recognize that you are going to feel an array of emotions. This is a good time to give yourself a break from functioning at your usual high levels of energy and allow yourself to lean on your support system.

When going through my divorce, I found distance to be an important factor. I felt it would provide me the space to grieve, heal, and move on. I didn't want to see or talk to my ex-husband for a good six months because when I did, the cycle of hurt and pain would come back, leaving me in my emotions of despair all over again. Dealing with the divorce process meant that there had to be some communication over the paperwork, and we had kids together. In my desperation to gain the space I felt I needed, I ended up filing a restraining order against my ex-husband because I needed the space. He just kept coming around trying to talk to me. It forced me to file what felt like a false restraining order because he wasn't violent; it was more like emotional abuse. I could not handle it emotionally. I then disappeared with the kids for about 9 months before he finally found me. Space did help me get over him and find someone new in my life. Divorce does not provide that space totally because of the things that require both of you to figure out, so you have to communicate regardless of the hurt you are experiencing. Though I did not handle that situation in the best way, it was the way I coped with my hurt.

I think the best way to get over someone is to cut off all communication; that means texting, calling, and connections on social media. When you are not in the same space, you won't be tempted to be curious about the other person and focus your attention on moving forward. Unfortunately, this can't totally happen in a divorce situation, but it is possible in a Social Marriage. With Social Marriage, the legal system has no part in the relationship; that is, only where you involve them. Not having a marriage license can make the breakup a smoother process as far as paperwork. Unfortunately, there is still the hurt to address, and that takes time.

Palimony

Palimony is a term we don't hear a lot about. It was used by a celebrity divorce attorney, Marvin Mitchelson, back in 1977. You may be much more familiar with the term alimony that involves a person providing financial support for a spouse before or after separation or divorce. Palimony refers to couples who are cohabiting, not legally married. It is the division of property and finances when they breakup. It is not a formal or legal term. Some states may consider it in couple disputes where proof is provided in oral, implied (trends of payments or deposits into a person's account are viewed as patterns), or written form.

The Marvin v. Marvin case brought the situation of cohabiting to be considered in a different light. While plenty of people seem to enjoy the comforts of living together romantically without a marriage license, it can become a difficult situation when one person has been dependent on the other financially, and then they breakup, as with the Marvin v. Marvin case. While the court can't award you anything for your performance of sex for the time you voluntarily engaged in the relationship, it can look at property acquired and earnings of the couple during their time together. To decide, the court may need to view documents and other ways to conduct the relationship. When one person in the relationship feels they are owed something for their time and performance during the time of togetherness, it makes it difficult to just walk away empty-handed. It is recommended that if a couple decides to live romantically unmarried that they enter a legal cohabitation agreement. In a Social Marriage, the same rules apply. The emphasis is always on communication every step of the way.

There is the hope of the prenup and postnup for married couples that may offer some mental assurance for the person who wants to protect their finances and assets going into a relationship. The only problem is neither gets filed or shown to a judge until a divorce is filed. If the judge feels it is not reasonable, he will set it aside.

In most cases with Social Marriage, after you have lived together for a while, the couples know who is paying for the groceries or other bills without it being a conversation. The only way it becomes a legal battle is if someone wants revenge for whatever reason. But for the most part, if the two people want to break up mutually, then they don't try to cause each other any problems.

<u>Know What You're Walking Away From</u>

Walking away from a relationship may be easier when there is no legal action that needs to occur, just have a clear understanding of what you're walking away from. Once you part ways, there is the hurt to deal with, so your focus may not be gaining clarity of the breakup. If you are one that believes there are life lessons in every misfortune, then exploring and processing the experience can lead to learning, self-improvement, and even building a better life. Some may feel that thinking over the details is infuriating and causes them to be upset. But though this can be part of the process, the point of knowing what you're walking away from is to help you let go and move on.

Breakup and divorce don't just happen on paper. There is the process of letting go of the dreams you shared, how you connected intimately, and in some cases, the loss of a long-time friend and confidant. When you walk away from the mental perspective, you know what you walk away from the good and bad. It is more of a place of lessons learned and that the story you shared is over.

Some consideration should be given to a situation where children are involved. Walking away can't happen, at least not totally. The couple's relationship may be over, but they will always be connected through the kids. There will be co-parenting, weekend visitations, birthday parties, graduations, and weddings throughout the kids' life until adulthood. In a very real sense, you will always be family because of the kids. This may be a challenging situation to face when you part on bad terms. It calls for the couple to get their issues resolved for the sake of the kids. If I were thinking about my kids, the decisions I made during my divorce would not have been so selfish. My focus was on my own hurt, not what my kids needed. When parents bad mouth each other in front of the kids, it can build a conflicting image in their mind and influence how they interact with each parent or just one. Regardless of the saying, "sticks and stones may break my bones, but words will never hurt me," the reality is words hurt worse than sticks and stones.

Walking away from a relationship is not what most of us focus on in the beginning when things are going great. No matter if it is a legal marriage or Social Marriage, it can be difficult to just walk away. Healing takes time, and we all have our way of dealing with the pain. When you love someone, you are full of hope of what that relationship could be. As hard as I know it is, you can still have hope; the current chapter of your life is just ending. Knowing what you are walking away from allows you to eliminate all the second-guessing about what you should have done or not done. It allows you to be honest about why it didn't work out and accept the decision to part ways. The next chapter unwraps the elements of love that can be helpful before seeking out relationships. Whether or not you do the paperwork when a relationship ends, love is lost, and you still must face what you are walking away from. It's an internal process of letting go.

Chapter 7

UNDERSTANDING

LOVE

—⁓⁓⁓⁓—

Introduction

Love is more than "liking someone a lot" or tolerating them only when things are going well. The emotions that are felt when you first meet evolve over time as the relationship develops. Each person in the relationship owes it to themselves and their partner to be self-aware of their view of love and marriage. Love is not something you wait to experience when you get married; you bring it as your contribution. It should happen beforehand, with loving yourself. It's true that before you can love someone else, you must first love yourself. Having a need for love could be mistaken for having love to give. This is a deception that stems from a lack of self-awareness and knowledge of what love is.

This chapter goes deeper into what it takes for any marriage to survive. It boils down to how you understand love and your contribution to the other. Marriage is a selfless act that often ends when someone becomes selfish. The breakdown of the relationship can happen slowly or fast, depending on the personalities of the couple. The challenge for the relationship is to be present mentally and physically. Pay attention to the small and big shifts in thoughts and behaviors. Some things can be resolved with communication between the couple, while others may need a third-party professional to offer guidance.

Self-Love

Self-love is an important first step in any relationship. You first must love yourself before you can know how to love someone else. Some people think you have to find a partner to complete you. That is their mentality. But it should not be that way. It should be two people that are complete when they come together. Many people forget about self-love; they just love their partner or try to take care of everyone else around them. If they are not taking of themselves, they cannot effectively take care of those around them. It's the prime set up for a disaster later. Each person brings their own set of issues to the relationship, and there is no requirement for the other person to fix them for you. Seek to love yourself and do what it takes to heal from your issues to give your best to the relationship.

Some of us were never taught how to love ourselves. Most psychologists agree that many people learn to love themselves by first being loved by someone else. This probably sounds like I am contradicting myself but hear me out. Our family is the first set of people that surround us from growing up. If our family didn't show us love or make us feel lovable, then most likely, our self-esteem would be affected. The result will lead to us not knowing how to love ourselves as well as seeking out that love from others. In cases like those, a person has to discover that they are worthy of love. It is good if the person can reach that point before they get involved in a relationship. Otherwise, the relationship's initial focus would be getting that self-love need met instead of contributing to the pot of love you both dip in. That would mean there would need to be a practice and understanding of what self-love is. One way that I practice self-love is to create a vision board for myself that includes different categories such as careers, health, community, relationships, friends, and for each category, I would put my goals. I consider this self-love even though it has a relationship in it. The majority of it is circled around me and what I want to accomplish. This is a reminder that I matter and am worthy of the things I place on the vision board.

With the vision board, it can include steps or just have the goals. The law of attraction can still manifest your desires because your focus on behavior and thinking is committed. I also have a gratitude journal that I keep on my nightstand. Every morning I write down 3 things that I want to accomplish that day. I also write down affirmations for the day, for example, "I am a powerful and confident woman." Then at the end of the day, I write down 3 things that I am thankful for and review the things I wanted to accomplish. I found that 99% of the time, I accomplished what I wrote down. For me, that means I had a good day because the top 3 things I wanted happened. I am also not ignorant of the fact that my effort played a role in it.

A sacrifice contribution slowly cuts away at the relationship. This starts off with someone taking care of or helping the other person somehow as they put something for themselves on hold. As time goes on, one or both persons may become bitter and use it as a reason to feel unappreciated or be right. Most likely, neither individual will feel good about the sacrifice. The best-case scenario is when the contributions flow out of love and not from the obligation of sacrifice. The relationship is about give-and-take, not making it all about the other person, and then get bitter about it. Again, as I have said throughout this book, communication is key. If you want something, it should be communicated.

Types Of Love

There are several ways to love someone according to the relationship you have with them. Explore your feelings for those in your life. How do you understand love? With couples, there are more intimate elements of love to consider. In my previous chapters, I talked about the 5 love languages and how learning your partner's love language can help you love them the way they want to be loved. I encourage couples to take the 5 love languages quiz to at least open up the discussion. The quiz can be found at 5lovelaguages.com. It only takes about ten minutes to answer about 25 questions for the couple's part. You can't give the same love to your partner as you give to yourself. It is also important to know that your love language evolves. People do change and even grow apart if too much time passes without communication. This is one of the reasons that marriage is work because you must communicate through different changes. You must communicate to be on the same page. This is why I think counseling is important. People may not know what to talk about, but the help of a third-party professional can offer guidance in what to do to get the couple back on track.

The ancient Greeks defined 8 different love types. But do keep in mind that while it is important to be familiar with the different love types, it is more important to know that your partner needs a certain kind of love. Even if their love language is not physical touch, that does not mean you can skip being intimate with them. Your partner is more than family, so they need a different love than what you would give to family or your child. The following list can be found in literature and in different places on the world wide web. The point in showing them is to make you aware of the different types of love and their meanings. Family members are many, and the significant other, there is only one. Conflicts arise when the wrong type of love encroaches in the wrong relationships.

- **Philia.** An affectionate Love. This love has been referred to as brotherly love, where people share deep friendships or are family.
- **Pragma.** It is said to be enduring love. This love is a maturing love that develops over time and has a purpose. It can be between a couple who are dedicated and committed to each other.
- **Storge.** Known as familial love. It's a love between parents and their children.
- **Eros.** A romantic love where the couple engages in physical touch and pleasure.
- **Ludus.** A playful kind of love that can be expressed through flirting.
- **Mania.** Or obsessive love, the focus is more on self than the other person.
- **Philautia.** This is a type of self-love where the person appreciates themself.
- **Agape.** A selfless love that involves empathy for everyone.

The goal of the couple is an area that some couples don't discuss. It may not seem like a big deal until they start drifting apart when their goals change, or one person doesn't have goals, and the other does. Goals need to be aligned even if they are not the same goals. There should be something that compliments the other person, but most of all, each person's goal should be supported by the other.

■ The Wrong Way to Love

Unfortunately, some people experience love yet another way when they are loved by a narcissist person. This can make it challenging to know what love is when one is not familiar with the personality disorder. Narcissists have a different perspective on not just love but on life itself. Here I just want to share a little information about what may be experienced in the love area for you to look for. The web offers plenty of articles on the disorder to better understand narcissism if you want more reading. The information here comes from Psychology Today.

Narcissists have a grand view of themselves and will remind their intimate partners of how good they are. They are preoccupied with fantasies of unlimited success, power, brilliance, beauty, or ideal love. This can be hurtful to a relationship because they are preoccupied with everything being about them. So, things are good as long as you make them look good but as soon as you point out any imperfections, there is a problem. You run the risk of becoming the enemy. The relationship with a narcissist is not give-or-take. There is a level of deception, though, as long as they receive constant admiration. Whatever they do has to be praised to no end; meanwhile, your needs are not getting met. Narcissists have a way of always putting their needs first, and they are right all of the time. If something is wrong, it must be the other person's fault because they do things perfectly. Remember how you love yourself should not hurt your partner.

I provided just a glimpse into the traits of a narcissist. There are more. The main point is for you to recognize the patterns that only get worse. If you notice that your partner is causing you to doubt yourself, and in the relationship, nothing is good unless they are right and things go their way, you may be dealing with a narcissist. Because narcissism is a spectrum of symptoms, it may be difficult to separate the pieces. I always recommend counseling with a professional who has more insight into the disorder and can offer guidance to both individuals.

Meaning Behind The Marriage Vows

I have been to a few weddings and found that marriage vows seem to be taken less seriously during the marriage ceremony. Writing your own vows is beginning to be a popular thing to do. In some cases, it appears that the couples are trying to be more entertaining for the audience than committing to the relationship in a meaningful way. I have heard someone say as their vow that they would allow their partner to watch as much football as they like. They only address the light-hearted things and don't address the things that will get them through the rough spots of a marriage. I am convinced that the marriage ceremony is more for family and friends. The couples that are eloping are not focused on showing an audience anything. They seem more interested in sharing that moment with each other. A lot of money and effort is spent in a marriage ceremony to make friends and family happy when in reality, when the couple has problems in their relationship later friends and family stay away and do nothing to try and help the couple stay together.

After doing some digging, I found the evolution of marriage ceremonies and the marriage vows have come a long way. But not just that: the meaning didn't begin as wholesome and religious as you might be thinking. The marriage union in times past - with the ancient Greeks, Hebrews, and Romans -

didn't have love as the focus. It was more about the man owning the woman as someone to bear his offspring to be sure they were his biological heirs. Polygamy and concubines were acceptable in those times and served to satisfy the man's sexual urges and impulses. It wasn't until the Middle Ages that love became a driving force in marriage. Some believe it was perhaps introduced by the French. Religion entered the picture by way of the Roman Catholic church in the eighth century. The Priest played a crucial role in making the marriage legal. Things took another turn when women won the right to vote. They were no longer viewed as property but as equals. That was just in the 1960s. The first recorded marriage ceremony goes back about 2350 B.C. in Mesopotamia. Though the words of the traditional marriage vows can and have been picked apart to mean different things to different people, we can still agree that they are still losing the battle with keeping couples together. Just at face value, we can examine some of the vows for a deeper meaning.

"Till death do us part" - now means until divorce, or until "I'm unhappy to do my part." Apparently, in some people's minds, a concept like faithfulness is not a given. Again, communication, even counseling, can be helpful.

"In good or bad times" - being there for the good and bad times is a commitment that depends on the character, nature, or personality of the couple involved. The task is knowing how each of you handles stress in different areas of your life and being there for each other no matter how bad things get.

"In sickness and health" - the challenge is, are you capable of caring for someone when they are sick and not at their best? Always know your limitations, sometimes life presents these situations.

"To love and honor" - having a marriage license doesn't make loving and honoring someone an automatic instance, and neither does just living together. The idea is that you come into the marriage with love and honor in your heart, ready to provide it. Because it started with you loving and honoring yourself.

These vows are said to come from a book called the Book of Common Prayer. We have received it as religious text that means something we can stand by. But like many of us know, the divorce statistics are still going up. This can only mean that a true understanding of love is called for. In the next and final chapter, I hope to take you just a bit deeper into where I feel our responsibility lies. We have been given information over time that lacks the meaning we assumed it did. It is now time that we reassess and reflect on something more.

Chapter 8

TRUE COMMITMENT VERSUS A PIECE OF PAPER

$\sim\!\!\infty\!\!\sim\!\!\infty\!\!\sim$

Introduction

Your commitment to someone doesn't start with a piece of paper. It begins with what is in your heart. My current husband and I socially married nine years ago and are still going strong today. Yes, we have had our ups and downs just like any other relationship, but we work hard at it, we are committed to each other, and we don't give up. We don't need a legal document to prove our commitment or to end it because we understand the true proof is what we put into the relationship to keep it thriving. I have heard of different cases where a couple is happy together for many years, then they get married, and problems arise that test their happiness. In those moments, they start questioning if the marriage can last. There are also those cases where a couple has been married for years but have gone their separate ways within the marriage only committed on paper. Whatever the case may be, there should always be communication with the couple on the relationship's status and commitment.

Social Marriage is just as challenging as a legal marriage. The legal document is just that; it doesn't magically make the marriage work. I think some people may have higher expectations after they get the paper, but that will only take you down the path of disillusionment. The work of understanding commitment should begin before a commitment is made and include the work of self-awareness and one's fears.

With this last chapter, I emphasize the importance of understanding commitment as well as the control we each possess over our lives. Beyond the words "Yes" and "I do," there is the expectation of something big, almost magical in a sense. But while we hope for the best, we must also not neglect the focus and effort it takes to have the best. Building a life with the one you love is exciting. My goal is to share how it can be done in the most rewarding way possible.

Love Listens

When you are committed to someone, there is the work of listening. In order for a couple to know how to give to each other, they must listen to each other. I know this isn't happening with couples because the divorce rates are going up along with the number of clients in my office. When problems surface in a relationship, love listens. It is not quick to respond or defend. It listens first.

I recall a time when I was participating in a Family Feud game. One of the questions that came up was, "What are the top five questions a woman in a relationship wishes her man would ask her on a regular basis?" Everyone was guessing, "I love you" and some other responses but not getting the answer right. The number one thing out of the five things a woman wanted to hear was, "How was your day?" I thought, what a simple question, but yet men and husbands don't think to ask it on a daily basis. We would love to tell them about our day as a way to release, just to have them listen. Then I thought maybe the question is too loaded. It wasn't simple enough to just get a quick answer and move on. But in all fairness, we could ask men about their day and be there to listen as well. It could be a sharing moment. It truly could be an opportunity to engage in active listening, not a time for pretending to hear or zone out and think about something else. Then to demonstrate listening, there could be a response that begins with, "I hear what you're saying," or "How did that make you feel?" Often,

I think when women start talking, it could be about something that happened to them at work. When men respond, it's as if the women asked them to come up with a solution and save them when that is not the case. We just need them to listen to us. I get it; couples may not learn the art of listening right away. None of us do. We need time to see the patterns and learn about each other. I am not saying all men act the same way or all women do either because we are all unique individuals.

I do think it is true that men and women can be in the same space and not hear each other. Not just in the disagreeable sense but in a normal, casual, everyday encounter. Do I believe they love each other during those times? Of course. Their focus is different, though. Working through this is the key to an effective Social Marriage, legal marriage, or long-term togetherness relationship. To achieve success, there must be listening. And you should know that it is not only done by hearing. It involves studying your partner's behavior and noting patterns in how they do things. Learning generally about the differences between men and women is a good place to start; just be sure to take it a step further to understand your own partner.

According to marriage expert Mark Gungor, men and women have different brains. Women's brains are like a ball of wires connected to everything and driven by their emotions. It is why we can focus on many things at once. When women are stressed most of the time, they just want men to listen unless they ask for more. On the other hand, men have separate boxes representing their brains, and the boxes are not connected. Therefore, they can only focus on one thing at a time. They also have something called a "nothing box." The nothing box really has nothing in it. It is where men go to escape when they are stressed, and the reason they can do things like flick through channels for what seems like hours. The talk of the differences between men and women has been around and said in different ways for years. Here I just want to remind you of what you are up against as you create ways to engage and listen to each other. Below are some of the top points made in *Psychology Today* on what the opposite sexes want from one another.

■ What Women Want

- **A devoted, loving man.** This is not in words only but in actions too. His devotion should be demonstrated when the couple shares with her work, family, and friends.
- **Honesty.** Honesty in thoughts and whereabouts is helpful because women don't have to depend on their imagination for answers.
- **Generous spirit**. A generous man is refreshing. And they understand reciprocity.
- **Satisfying Sex.** This area can be different for everyone, but what makes it satisfying is when a man knows what his woman wants.

■ What Men Want

- **Sex.** Men may think about sex more than women think. Don't confuse this with romance, just sexual desire.
- **Freedom.** Too many demands or questions can make a man feel trapped or boxed in.
- **Forgiveness.** Believe it or not, holding grudges, according to some men, sends off an alert that makes them concerned.
- **Appreciation.** Men like being stroked and told how much they are appreciated.

It is important to know that regardless of these highlighted differences, some people are drawn to each other because of a need met for the moment. Keyword, "moment." So, in your quest to know if the person you are with is committed, ask yourself are they listening to you totally or just taking care of one of your needs temporarily, which happens to be one of their needs? Something to think about.

Commitment Stays

Commitment to a person goes beyond a piece of paper. It is a bond that works to gain clarity for the purpose of staying together. Experiencing disagreements and problems are a part of life, we all have them, but can we stay committed during the process? There are folks out there that want to feel those butterflies with every encounter in their relationship. They want to feel it when they wake up in the morning. I found that those people are still single. In my opinion, I don't feel that is the correct way of thinking about it. I say while at the beginning of a relationship, you may feel butterflies, even at different moments, but still, love is a daily choice you need to make. Every day when you wake up, you make a choice to be with the person you are with - or not. And it is a constant commitment over and over again. The more days you stay committed, the stronger the relationship is.

I remember in a transformation class I attended, they asked us, "What is a 100% commitment?" They had this acronym, O.W.T.F.G.F.I.A. Pretty long, right? It is interpreted as, "Oh, What the Fuck Go For It Anyway." I laughed at first, but how accurate! No matter what, you stay with the initial commitment. That is 100% commitment. You don't allow anything to get in the way of that. Relationships are not bulletproof on their own; the couple has to make it that way. Every hurt feeling or disagreement should not test your commitment to each other. There should be an expectation that those things will happen sometimes. You both are two unique individuals with your own way of doing things, and sometimes you will clash. Love does not make you hurt the other person intentionally. Even misunderstandings go back to communication.

You are committed to the whole of what the relationship is, the good and the bad. We all have flaws, so you don't get to pick out the pieces you want and leave the rest. Life is a combination of ups and downs. I don't think there is a way to get around it. It's just like the Covid-19 pandemic we are in the midst of; it is just one of those unfortunate interruptions. Unfortunately, some relationships have not been able to handle it. The divorce rate during this pandemic is at an all-time high. People are seeking legal counsel on how to be apart. It is reported that even in China, divorce cases have increased by 25%. The reason for this is said to be trivial matters that have escalated to conflicts and poor communication. Stressful situations have a way of showing what we are made of. The negative times often show our true character. It is not just divorce that has spiked in numbers. Other negatives, like child abuse and domestic violence, have as well. It seems couples are allowing the stress of unemployment and other negative factors to affect their relationships. The reality is we don't all respond to stress in the same way. Some people take this time to spend quality time and reconnect with family, while others use it to fight or argue more. You really can't blame it on the situation because it is the same for all of us. It boils down to the individual and how they handle stress.

I find it interesting how some couples will boast six months into the relationship about how smooth things are going, no arguments or anything. That tells me that they have not experienced any conflict. I think conflict is good in the way that it shows how each person handles it. The sooner this happens, the better. I would even say ask the hard questions when you begin dating or before marriage during counseling. You need someone you can weather the storms of life with, that is, if you choose to be in a relationship.

<u>Your Control</u>

Knowing where you have control is key to your survival in a legal or Social Marriage. You can only control yourself, not the other person. It helps to understand compatibility and know your expectations before you enter any relationship. Social Marriage gives people that continued control. They have the ability to separate or divorce in the least stressful way possible when divorce is inevitable. Like I mentioned before, it is already a stressful situation without the added lawyer fees and paperwork. I know Social Marriage isn't for everyone, but there is more to consider than worrying about having a piece of paper or not.

Throughout this book, you have read about all that it takes to be in a meaningful relationship. In the beginning, I shared my own story and the challenges I faced trying to sever the legal relationship with my ex-husband. The result of my pain led me to find a way to control my own situation. Social Marriage was born out of that pain. The process is not that different than a legal marriage. I hope you can see where I have been persistent with trying to get you to see the deeper picture of togetherness, commitment, and all that it takes to have a relationship that nurtures and grows with the couple as they learn each other. The problems that end marriages are many. Finding solutions to negative situations like ending a marriage is not easy. When the couple decides to part ways even after trying all the things that are supposed to work to keep them together, what is next? How do you make a negative not so negative? My thought is Social Marriage. Self-gratification is the driving force that is behind a lot of selfish acts that lead to divorce. I want to help take some of the stings out of that. But it requires a lot of self-work as well as couple-work.

I have mentioned quite strongly the control you have over doing what it takes to stay in the relationship. Please allow me to briefly go in the opposite direction of using your control to walk away from a relationship. When a relationship is toxic, being in it can be damaging to your person. In a relationship, you must know when it is not good. Abuse of any type is not good. I just wanted to make that clear because for some, that is what they have been told is love and to leave is not good. When I talked about self-love in another chapter, I stated that you must know how to love yourself before loving another. Self-love speaks to how you value yourself. If someone is not showing that they value you, well, that is not love.

In conclusion, I hope to now leave you with your eyes wide open and minds stimulated. I am not here to convince you that you should be in a relationship. Relationships are wonderful when they work. It is when they don't when things get hectic. Again, everybody can't handle the pressure. But for those who can, I encourage you. Every day you can make a choice to love and be committed. It has very little to do with a legal document. It is only a matter of the heart.